Make Your Own Merry Christmas

This book shows you how to make the most of *your* Christmas, through jokes, games, tricks and things to make. There's something here for every member of the family to enjoy. And for the grand finale, there's a special panto to perform!

BROUGH GIRLING

Make Your Own Merry Christmas

Cartoons by Tony Blundell
Illustrations by Chris Evans

A Magnet Book

First published in 1987 as a Magnet paperback original
by Methuen Children's Books Ltd
11 New Fetter Lane, London EC4P 4EE
Text copyright © 1987 Brough Girling
Cartoons copyright © 1987 Tony Blundell
Illustrations copyright © 1987 Chris Evans

Printed in Great Britain
by Cox & Wyman Ltd, Reading

British Library Cataloguing in Publication Data

Girling, Brough
  Make your own merry Christmas. ——— (A
  Magnet book).
  1. Christmas ——— Juvenile literature
  I. Title
  790.1   GT4985

  ISBN 0-416-06482-5

Contents

Introduction   7

Making Them Laugh!   9
  Stand Up Comedy   9
  Double Acts   13
  'Here is the News'   16
  The Oldest Joke in the History of the World!   23
  Doctor Doctor Jokes   25
  Short Sketches and Jokes   28
  Knock Knock Jokes   33
  Policemen Jokes   35
  Waiter Jokes   37
  Three Man Sketches – Dog Jokes!   39
  Taking the Micky!   42

Christmassy Things to Make and Do   45
  Make Your Own Decorations   45
  Special Effects – the Easy Way!   52
  Personalise the Party!   56
  Make Your Own Silent Crackers   58
  Make Your Own Christmas Wrapping Paper   64
  Make Your Own Christmas Cards   67

Games for One and All   71
  Racing Games   71
  Moderately Quiet Games   76
  Quiet Games Round a Table   79
  Harmless Practical Jokes   82
  Games That Turn Out To Be Practical Jokes   86

Conjuring, Card Tricks and Puzzles 89
Man of Mystery's Marvellous Memory Trick 89
Conjuring Tricks To Do 92
A Tricky Story 98
A Party Puzzler 99
Crafty Card Tricks 102

Longer Jokes 107
Gorilla in a Pub 107
Three-Legged Turkeys 109
Toilet Water! 110

A Potted Panto For Four Performers 112

Introduction

ONCE UPON A TIME, not very long ago, people didn't have televisions.

This meant that when families and friends got together to enjoy themselves they made their own entertainment. I think there's little doubt that a lot of the entertainment they made would have been very boring – with long songs from aunts, and nephews playing terrrible violin solos!

But at Christmas it can be different. This is because at Christmas time everyone is allowed to be very silly! Adults pretend that Christmas is a time for children (it isn't – it's for everyone!) and so we are all allowed to enjoy ourselves even if it means being daft. We can bring out the very best old jokes and tricks and games. Hurrah!

This book shows you how to do it. All you need to do is read it and decide how you are going to use things in it to help you to make yourselves a very Merry Christmas.

Oh yes, and don't forget – turn off the telly!
Merry Christmas!

Making Them Laugh!

The most essential feature of any Merry Christmas is people laughing. It's quite easy to make people laugh, especially at a Christmas gathering or family party. This section shows you how to get started.

▶▶ Stand Up Comedy ◀◀

One of the oldest ways of raising a laugh is joke-telling, and the simplest form of telling jokes is to stand up and tell them! The

Victorian music halls, where people went for an evening of mixed entertainments, always had 'stand up' comedians. Their acts were called 'routines'. Routines are really just a string of good jokes.

There are two essential things to think about if you are going to be a successful stand up comedian.

The first is that it is always best to learn your routine off by heart – and to practise it until you can do it perfectly. If you find it difficult to learn by heart then you can use cards to help you remember which joke comes next. It is better to do without cards, and it never really works if you have to read out the jokes.

The other important thing is to get your 'timing' right. This means that you must leave time at the end of jokes for your audience to laugh, and you must 'pace' the jokes so that you get as many laughs as possible. It is impossible to show you how to do this in a book, and the best way to learn it is to watch someone who is very good at it. A good example is Ronnie Corbett telling one of his famous long jokes on *The Two Ronnies*.

You will see how Ronnie Corbett tells the story *slowly* – it's very tempting to gabble jokes, especially if you are feeling nervous or are trying to remember what comes next.

He also slows down, or stops, depending on how the audience is reacting: he always allows plenty of time for the joke to sink in, and for them to have a giggle at it! In order to do that you need to be sensitive to an audience, and you need to know your comic material inside out! So get practising!

Here is a short routine which should go down well at any Christmas party or family gathering. Add some favourite jokes of your own to it, but try to make it flow, so that one joke follows on from the next.

As it was Christmas I went to get a job at the butcher's the other day. The butcher said to me, 'Are you any good at maths?'

I said, 'Yes!'

He said, 'If a turkey weighed ten pounds, at 20p a pound, what would it be?'

I said, 'Bad.'

He said, 'That's right – you've got the job!'

· · ·

The first morning I worked there a lady came in with a bundle. 'Hey!' she said. 'I bought this turkey from you yesterday for Christmas and there's something wrong with it!'

'What?' I asked.

'It's dead!' she said.

· · ·

That reminds me – did you hear about the little boy who asked his mother if he could have a puppy for Christmas? 'No,' she said. 'You can have turkey like everyone else!'

• • •

Last year I asked Mum if I could have a sledge. She said yes, but that I'd have to share it with . . . (*use the name of your brother, or cousin or friend – preferably someone in the room*). So I do – I use it going downhill, and he has it for the uphill bits!

• • •

I went with Mum to the toyshop this year. She said to the man behind the counter, 'I want something for my son.' (*daughter, if you're a girl!*)
   He said, 'How much were you thinking of asking?'
   She said, 'No, I mean a toy, for Christmas.'
   He said, 'I see, well here's a nice one.'
   She said, 'OK, that will do.'
   He said, 'Shall I wrap it up, or is he (*she*) going to smash it here?'

• • •

I'll finish with a definition of Christmas: it's the time when kids like me stop thinking of the past, and think of the *present*.
   Thank you.

12

Double Acts

Jokes and sketches done by two performers are a very old and very successful form of comedy. Laurel and Hardy, Morecambe and Wise and the Two Ronnies are marvellous examples of successful double acts.

Traditionally there was one 'funny man', and the other character was known as the 'straight man' or 'stooge'. The stooge usually set up the jokes and the funny man delivered the punch-lines and did a lot of clowning around. Ernie Wise was often 'straight man' to Eric Morecambe, who got most of the laughs.

In any such double act, however, both comics have to work equally hard. Timing lines to get the maximum laughs, and

13

establishing the right characters so that comedy can flourish, is an art of which the people mentioned above were, and are, masters.

Here are some double act jokes for you to practise. They should be just right for performing to a friendly Christmas audience! It is an advantage in any double act for the two characters to look very different from each other. Notice how with the examples of Laurel and Hardy, Morecambe and Wise and the Two Ronnies, one of them is always much bigger than the other! Try to team up with someone who is a very different shape from you!

It is important to learn double act routines off by heart, and to practise until you are word perfect.

This easy little routine takes the micky out of Mum and Dad, but you could easily adapt it to fit an uncle and aunt, or anyone else in your audience who can take a joke!

Have you ever seen a man-eating shark?
No, but last Christmas I saw a man eating turkey! – my dad!

• • •

Did you know that my dad's an exporter?
No.
He is – he's an ex-British-Rail-porter!

• • •

Oh! My dad's got a leading job in a circus.
  Has he?
  Yes, he leads in the lions!

• • •

I asked Dad to give me a bike for Christmas.
He said he couldn't afford it, but I pointed out
that it would save him money.
  How?
  Well, it would stop me wearing out my
shoes so quickly!
  *My dad's very mean too. He gave my mum
some flowers for Christmas.*
  What sort?
  *We don't know – they haven't even started
to come up yet!*

• • •

My dad was going to
give me a pocket
calculator but I told him
not to bother.
  Why?
  Well I already know
how many pockets I've
got!
  *Mine gave me a watch
last year. It was
waterproof and
shockproof.*
  Why don't you wear it?
  It caught fire!

That reminds me – my mum tried to make a Christmas cake this year.
What went wrong?
The candles melted in the oven!
I reckon my mum's getting short-sighted.
Why?
Last night she was sitting down looking at the glass door of the washing-machine.
What for?
She thought Dad's shirts going round and round was the wrestling on the telly!
Did she really? Tell you what – let's go down the launderette and watch a film!

Exit – fast!

▶▶   'Here is the News'   ◀◀

A very successful way to present unconnected jokes is to do a 'take-off' of the news on TV. You can do these by yourself, or with an accomplice.

All you need to do is sit behind a table or desk, like a TV newscaster, and what makes these sketches particularly good to do is that you don't need to learn anything – you just read the jokes from sheets of paper.

Here are some jokes to start you off on Christmas Eve; on the next pages there are routines for Christmas Night and Boxing Day!

If you are doing them with two newscasters, just take alternate jokes, but practise to make sure you know who is doing what, and always allow time between jokes for the laughs. This means not coming in too quickly when it's your turn.

▷ Here is the News for Christmas Eve ◁

A small boy was taken to hospital today complaining that he is very frightened of Father Christmas coming down the chimney tonight. A hospital spokesman says they suspect he is suffering from Santa Claustrophobia.

• • •

Father Christmas got out of bed early today and asked his wife what the weather was like. She looked out of the window and said, 'It looks like reindeer.'

17

A ton of glue has spilled from a lorry on the M1; police are asking drivers to stick to their own lanes.

• • •

An entire pack of foxhounds were stolen today in a remarkable robbery. Police say they have no leads.

• • •

A cowboy was arrested for eating a bag of sweets in a cinema today. Police say he was rustling.

• • •

As it's Christmas Eve many chickens were going cheep today.

• • •

And finally the weather forecast. It will be very cold this Christmas Eve, with temperatures falling to below zero degrees *Santagrade*.

Here is the News for Christmas Night

We are pleased to report that the siege at Dublin zoo is now over. The Irish police have shot all the gorillas, and released the 'ostrages.

• • •

A man in Brighton has successfully crossed an elephant with a Wilton. He's got a huge pile on his carpet.

• • •

Grotties, the high street shoe store, is offering a special deal on shoes when it re-opens tomorrow. Buy one shoe and they give you the other one free.

• • •

Someone crept into a house today while a family party was going on, and stole a pint of milk and a piece of fish from the fridge. Police think it may have been a cat burglar.

• • •

Mrs Lydia Dustbin, the lady with five legs, was given a new pair of knickers today. She says they fit her like a glove.

More news from the zoo: a hyena is reported to have swallowed a box of Oxo cubes. Its keeper said it has made a laughing stock of itself.

* * *

Sports news: Manchester United have just signed a new striker. He will play in their traditional red strip but insists on wearing black wellies and a cloak with a hood. It's believed he will play as Santa Forward.

And finally, a lorry loaded with hair restorer crashed on the M1 today. Police say they are combing the area.

▷ Here is the News for Boxing Day ◁

Good evening, here is the news this Boxing Day evening.

A lady got to the sales first thing this morning and bought a jumper. She brought it back at lunchtime complaining that there was a hole in it. The assistant told her that it was in polo-mint condition.

• • •

All the toilet seats were stolen today from Scotland Yard . . . The police say they have nothing to go on.

• • •

The voters at the Little Snodsbury by-election have returned a Conservative candidate – they say they'd like to exchange him for a better one.

• • •

A new deodorant went on sale for the first time today. It's called Vanish. When you spray it under your arms you disappear, and everyone wonders where that awful smell is coming from.

• • •

Another tale from today's sales: a woman
went into a store today and asked if she
could try on a dress in the window. The
assistant advised her to use the changing-
room instead.

• • •

Rare and precious birds escaped from an
aviary over the Christmas holiday. The
police say the theft is being looked into by
the flying squad.

• • •

A plastic surgeon fell into a fire today: he
melted.

• • •

A man was caught stealing money from a till
in a shop this afternoon. He told the police he
thought the change would do him good.

• • •

Now tonight's international football results:
Finland 3 Fatland 1.

▶▶ The Oldest Joke in the ◀◀ History of the World!

I don't really believe that 'Waiter! What's this fly doing in my soup?' is the oldest joke in the whole world, but it probably has more endings than any other joke in the English language.

I list a good number of 'punch-lines' below: I'm sure you can add some more. (A punch-line is the last line of a joke – the one that's supposed to get a laugh!)

You can perform these lines as a sketch. It would probably be best for one performer to sit at a restaurant table, and the other to come in as the waiter, and do the jokes very quickly, one after the other.

Here we go!

WAITER! WHAT'S THIS FLY DOING IN MY SOUP?

Breast stroke, sir!

I said it was meat and vegetable soup, sir!

I'm sorry, sir, I didn't know you were a vegetarian!

Keep quiet, sir, or they'll all want one!

Hang on, I'll bring him a spoon, sir!

So *that's* where they go in the winter!

Leave him if you've had enough, sir!

Could you eat round him, sir?

I suppose it's the mould he's after, sir!

I'm sorry, we don't allow pets in here, sir!

I don't expect he'll drink much of it, sir!

The DDT in it should kill him, sir!

I think he's committing insecticide, sir!

Don't worry, there's no extra charge, sir!

Isn't it sad to see them die, sir!

Don't worry, they usually sink when they die, sir!

They don't seem to care what they eat, sir!

Shall I give him the kiss of life, sir?

Our fly-strainer must be leaking, sir!

He won't live long in that stuff, sir!

It's not deep
enough to
drown him,
sir!

etc, etc! . . .

▶▶   Doctor Doctor Jokes   ◀◀

There are *hundreds* of Doctor Doctor jokes!
They are great for family gatherings at
Christmas. They can be told by a single
comedian – especially if he's feeling very
brave – but they are better as double acts.
One character must obviously be the doctor
– behind a desk, the other as the patient
comes in and goes out for every joke. They
are very corny, so deliver them nice and fast
before anyone can groan!   Here are a few of
my favourites:

Doctor Doctor, I think I've lost my memory!
When did it happen?
When did what happen?

Doctor Doctor, my eyesight isn't very good.
Let me see; you're suffering from double
vision!
*I'm not taking any notice of you two; I want a
third opinion!*

Doctor Doctor, I feel run down.
*Well, in future look both ways before you
cross the road.*

Doctor Doctor – it's terrible – I keep thinking
I'm a bell.
*Take these tablets and if you don't feel better
give me a ring.*

Doctor Doctor, if I get glasses will I be able
to read?
Of course you will.
Oh good, I've never been able to before!

Doctor Doctor, it's terrible. I'm losing my job through sickness.
Losing your job through sickness?!
Yes – my boss says he's sick of me!

Doctor Doctor, I don't like the idea of an operation.
Oh come now – you'll find it very amusing.
Will I?
Yes, it will leave you in stitches!

Doctor Doctor, I get this pain up my nose when I drink a cup of tea.
Have you tried taking the spoon out?

Doctor Doctor, my hair keeps falling out. Have you got anything to keep it in?
Yes. A paper bag!

There are quite a few jokes about doctors that you have to tell rather than act out. Here's a good one:

A man walked into a doctor's waiting-room with a large seagull standing on the top of his head. When the doctor was ready he called him in.

The doctor was amazed
when he saw the man.
'What seems to be the
trouble?' he asked. 'I've
got a man stuck to my feet,'
said the seagull!

▶▶ Short Sketches and Jokes ◀◀

Here is a small collection of comic sketches
and jokes for two actors. You could put them
into some of your double act routines, or
simply perform them on their own, as part of
a show, mixed perhaps with some conjuring
tricks, monologues or riddles.

First some really nonsensical ones. Act
them as if they make perfect sense to you:

1st Voice: Windy, isn't it?
2nd Voice: No, it's Thursday!
1st Voice: So am I. Let's go and have a drink!
Exit

• • •

1st Voice: Look – a flock of cows!
2nd Voice: It's not a flock, it's a herd.
1st Voice: Herd of what?
2nd Voice: Herd of cows.
1st Voice: Of course I've heard of cows.
2nd Voice: No, cow herd.
1st Voice: Don't you call me a coward!
Exit.

• • •

1st Voice: It's nice here, isn't it?
2nd Voice: Yes.
1st Voice: Have you lived here all your life?
2nd Voice: Not yet.
1st Voice: I've got it!
2nd Voice: Well don't give it to me!
1st Voice: I'm going to give you a piece of my mind!
2nd Voice: I didn't know you had any to spare!
Exit.

Did you hear about the cannibal who went away for a Christmas holiday and came back with big bits missing from his body?
No.
Yes, it was a self-catering holiday!
Well, I've heard about the cannibal who had a bad stomach ache.
Really?
Yes, he must have eaten someone who disagreed with him!
Exit.

• • •

Enter a lady.
Enter a man.
Man: I'm very sorry, I've just run over one of your chickens. I'd like to replace it.
Lady: I see, how many eggs do you lay a week?
Exit.

• • •

Enter a grumpy farmer.
Enter a tourist.
Tourist: Excuse me, I'd like to pick some fruit please.
Farmer: Push off!
Tourist: But that sign by your gate says 'Pick Your Own Fruit'!
Farmer: That's right – push off and pick yer own, you're not picking mine!
Exit.

Man rushing into a hardware store: Do you sell mousetraps?
Man behind counter: Yes, sir.
Ist man: Well, sell me one quickly, I've got a bus to catch.
Man behind counter: Oh, we don't sell any that big, sir!
Exit.

• • •

Enter two old farmers, both with very rustic voices.
First farmer: You know you said that when your cow was ill last week you gave it a gallon of cod-liver oil?
Second farmer (slowly): Yea!
First farmer: Well, my cow was ill yesterday, and I gave it a gallon of cod-liver oil, and it died!
Second farmer: That's funny . . . so did mine.
Exit.

• • •

Enter a doctor who sits behind a desk. A patient comes in.

Patient: I feel terrible, doctor.

Doctor: I see. Have you had treatment from any other doctor for it?

Patient: No, I've only been to the chemist.

Doctor: Chemist! What would that idiot know about it. What sort of ridiculous advice did the fool give you?

Patient: He told me to come and see you!

Exit.

• • •

Enter a shop assistant, stands behind counter. Enter a customer.

Customer: Good morning. I'd like a really expensive present for my wife for Christmas. (*say mother if the customer is a girl!*)

Assistant: I see. Well, we have some very, very expensive necklaces.

Customer: What are they made of?

Assistant: Alligators' teeth.

Customer: Alligators' teeth! I'd have thought that pearls would have been much more expensive than alligators' teeth.

Assistant: Oh no, sir. Any sissy can open an oyster!

Bow and exit.

▶▶ **Knock Knock Jokes** ◀◀

Knock Knock jokes really *must* be
performed by two people. It is ideal, of
course, if one of them is outside the room!
This also makes them very easy to do
because the person who has to start every
joke off is out of sight and can therefore read
them from a prepared list: there's very little
memorising to do. The person in the room
only has to say 'Who's there?' etc! Easy.

It's best to have the door ajar so that the
audience can hear clearly, but the person
outside the room may have to shout to make
sure the joke comes across.

Here's some to start you off – I'm sure you
know lots more:

1st voice (outside room): Knock knock!
Who's there?
Juno!
Juno who?
Juno what day it is?
Yes, Christmas Day! (*or Christmas Eve or whatever the date is*)

Knock knock!
Who's there?
Hosanna!
Hosanna who?
How's Sanna Claus going to get down our chimney – we've got central heating! (*adapt this to suit the circumstances – if it's Boxing Day say 'How Sanna Claus got down our chimney I'll never know . . . etc*)

Knock knock!
Who's there?
Little old lady!
Little old lady who?
I didn't know you could yodel!

Knock Knock!
Who's there?
Butcher.
Butcher who?
Butcher left leg in, yer left leg out, in out, in out, shake it all about!

Knock Knock!
Who's there?
Noah!
Noah who?
Noah any good knock knock jokes?!

34

▶▶ Policemen Jokes ◀◀

There are, of course, lots and lots of jokes
involving policemen! They often make very
good little two-man sketches and are
particularly funny if the person playing the
policeman has a helmet on – you can buy
these in joke or toy shops.

   Here are some jokes that you can act out as
double acts, or you could adapt them for
telling by one person if you want to.

Policeman: Excuse me, sir. Why were you
going so fast?
Motorist: Well, officer, this car hasn't got any
brakes, and I was hurrying home before I
had an accident!

• • •

Policeman: Excuse me, sir. Are you aware that this is a one-way street?
Motorist: But officer – I was only going one way!

• • •

Man: Officer! Officer! I've lost my little dog!
Policeman: Well why don't you put a notice in the newspaper about it?
Man: My dog can't read!

• • •

Man: Officer! Officer! I've just been robbed by two men!
Policeman: Can you give me a description of them, sir?
Man: Yes, one was six-feet six tall, and the other was a dwarf.
Policeman: Thank you, sir – we'll search high and low for them.

Waiter Jokes

There are some very good waiter jokes –
besides the fly in my soup ones on page 24
They are ideal as very short sketches done
by two people. Here are a few well-tried
ones:

Waiter waiter, do you have frog's legs?
No, sir, I always walk this way!
or
Waiter waiter, do you have frog's legs?
Yes, sir!
Well, hop off into the kitchen and get me a
steak!

Waiter waiter, does the band play requests?
Yes, sir.
Well, ask them to go and play in the traffic
until I've finished my meal!

• • •

Waiter, call me a taxi.
You're a taxi, sir!

• • •

Waiter, there's a slug in my salad!
I'm sorry, sir, I didn't know you were a
vegetarian.

38

Waiter: Now then, sir, how did you find your steak?
Man: Oh, I just moved a couple of chips and there it was!

▶▶ Three Man Sketches – ◀◀ Dog Jokes!

Here are some good jokes that you can act out, involving dogs. They are best done by three actors, one of whom is always the dog.

You could fit these jokes into other routines, or you could perform them one after the other.   Good luck!

A man and a dog enter, followed by a policeman.
Policeman: Has your dog got a licence?
Man: No, he's not old enough to drive!
Exit

• • •

A man and a dog enter, the man is holding a chessboard. He puts the chessboard down in front of the dog and quickly sets out the pieces. The dog and the man start playing chess!

A spectator enters and watches them for a moment or two, then he speaks.
Spectator: Why! That's amazing! A dog that plays chess! It's incredible – he must be brilliant!

Dog owner: It's not all that amazing – he's only won three of the last ten games!
Exit

A man is serving behind the bar in a pub – pretend to be cleaning glasses. An owner and his dog come in.

Owner: Do you know, this dog can talk!

Barman: Go on! I bet it can't! I bet you five pounds!

Owner: OK. You ask it anything you like and it will answer! Try!

Barman to dog: Good evening. How are you feeling?

Dog (bark out the answer): ROUGH!

Barman: I see. What do you call the top of a house?

Dog (barking again): ROOF!

Barman: OK then. Who was the manager of the England Football team that competed in the Mexico World Cup in 1986?

Dog (still barking); ROUGH!

Barman to Owner: Go on! What a load of rubbish! Give me my five pounds and get out!

The owner hands over five pounds and he and the dog start to walk out of the room. When you are nearly out, the dog must turn to the owner and say:

Oh, I remember now; it was Bobby Robson!

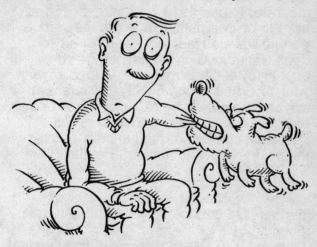

And finally, my favourite!

A man and his dog come in. The dog sits down quietly beside the man. A second man comes in and smiles at the dog as if wanting to make friends with it: then he says:

Does your little dog bite?

Second man: No.

The newcomer pats the dog, which snaps
viciously at him, snarls and barks.
Second man (holding his bitten fingers):
AAhhhh. You said your dog didn't bite!
First man: He doesn't. This isn't my dog!

▶▶ Taking the Micky! ◀◀

You can usually get what is called a 'cheap'
laugh – that is an easy laugh – if you tell jokes
that refer to people in your audience. You
have to be certain that they are the sort of
people who can take a joke. After all you
don't want blood on the carpet, do you,
especially at Christmas-time (especially not
your blood!). Making fun of someone is an
art, and it needs to be done as cheeky fun; it
mustn't be at all spiteful. Here are some
jokes that can be adapted to help you 'take
the micky' out of family and friends.

If your dad, or an uncle or brother likes fishing, adapt this story by using their names:

You know how Dad (*or whoever you want to name*) is very keen on fishing. Well, I don't think he's very bright about it. The other day he was out on . . . lake (*choose a local lake*) with a friend of his (*name someone if you can*). They had hired a boat and gone out into the middle. They rowed about a bit and then they started to catch quite a lot of fish – which is unusual for Dad. His mate said to him, 'It's very good here, will you remember this spot?' Dad said, 'I tell you what, I'll chalk a cross on the side of the boat so we'll know where it is in future.' 'Don't be daft,' said his mate, 'we might get a different boat next time!'

Here's one against someone who is mad on golf. Again, you can adapt it to suit any golfing members of your family, but I'll write it as if it's about your dad.

You know how my dad is very keen on golf, well my mum's been on at him about it.
    'Golf, golf, golf – is that all you ever think about?' she said to him.
    He was really surprised – he didn't expect to see her on the golf course at midnight!

How about this if a member of your family is a bit overweight?!

My teacher asked me the other day what I'm going to do when I'm as big as my mum. I said, 'Go on a diet!'
Or:
My mum's got this terrible herbal backache. She has to take herbal backache pills for it. Yes, and I think she thinks I've got a very rusty cod's liver; she keeps making me swallow cod-liver oil!
Or:
My brother's taken up weight training. He stands around and waits for trains!

Always think of ways of making jokes personal to your audience – it makes them think you've made them up for yourself! Even by using the name of your local paper you can get an extra giggle.

Christmassy Things to Make and Do

If you are going to devise your own entertainment at Christmas it also makes sense to make things like your own decorations too. This will help to make your Christmas extra-specially yours, and it will save you money too.

I have purposely not included any recipes in this section: the last thing Mum and Dad will want is you doing your own thing in the kitchen at Christmas-time!

▶▶ ## Make Your Own ◀◀
Decorations

It isn't difficult to make some jolly Christmas decorations of your own. All these ideas are easy to do, and won't take very long so there will still be time for you to learn all your jokes for the big day! Here we go:

▷ ## Glueless Paperchains ◁

I find that making up paperchains, particularly bought ones in packets, is OK for about the first mile, then you get bored. Also, you are bound to make a mistake and put two yellows together, or miss out a blue; and anyway, after about half an hour your tongue is so covered in glue that it sticks to the top of your mouth. Have no fear. Here is a solution to all your paperchain problems – Glueless Paperchains!

Take a strip or two of paper, between about 10 and 20cm wide. Brightly-coloured paper is best.
Cut slits in it like this:

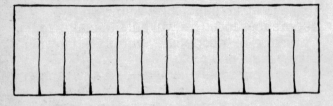

Now turn it round and cut similar slits along the opposite edge.

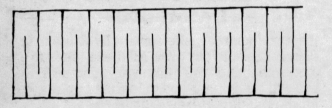

Now pull the ends apart with a twist. Look! Instant, glueless paperchains!

If you want to make a really long chain you can of course glue several of these strips together, but then they won't be glueless! A better and easier idea is to staple them with a small paper stapler.

You may be able to get round this problem altogether by making your glueless paperchains from a long strip of wallpaper. Use a pattern that is colourful, and cut your 10cm strips along the roll:

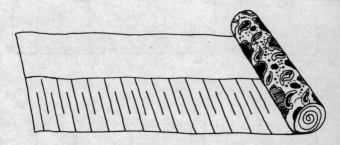

This way you'll have metres and metres of paperchain in minutes!

▷ Chinese Lanterns ◁

Chinese lanterns are easy to make, and if you put them up with your glueless paper-chains you will transform a room in no time!

Use brightly-coloured paper – Christmas wrapping paper is ideal, if you can afford it.

Start with a piece of paper about 15cm by about 25cm (it depends what size you want the lanterns to be)

Fold the paper in half.

Then fold up a flap about 3 or 4cm along both long edges.

Now make cuts about 2cm apart like this:

Don't cut through the flaps.

Open the paper out and glue, or staple, the paper into a tube.

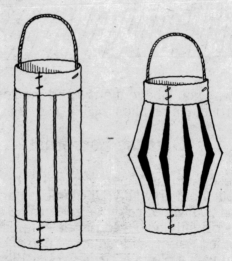

Push the top and bottom towards each other a little to form a lantern shape. Then glue or staple some string or coloured wool

to the top so that you can hang up your
Chinese lantern.

Window Stencils

Everybody dreams of a white Christmas
(except people like Australians, who like to
barbecue their turkeys on the beach).

Whether we have a white Christmas or not,
you can do your bit by spraying artificial
snow on your window-panes. If your dad is a
millionaire you can buy enough aerosols to
spray the whole garden, and his Rolls-Royce!

The normal way to decorate windows is to
make them look as if snow has blown into the
corners, like this:

You can also use stencils to make pictures
on the glass. There are good stencils of, for

49

example, snowmen and stars that you can buy, or you could make your own.

Here are some traditional ones, copy them to make your own stencils:

You can go one better than this by making silhouette portraits of members of the family, or people who may be coming to your Christmas party. These will have to be caricatures rather than actual portraits, so concentrate on particular features. If your

Uncle George is bald and smokes a pipe, make sure that his silhouette is very bald, and the pipe is very big. You can always add names if you have had difficulty with the likeness!

Christmas Candles

Candles are important at Christmas and there's an easy way to add a bit of sparkle to candles that you buy.

On a kitchen surface – out of Mum and Dad's way – or on a table protected with paper, sprinkle some Christmas 'glitter'. You can buy it in gold and silver, and several other colours.

Warm a candle simply by holding it in your hands for a while; all you are trying to do is to soften the outside of the wax a little.

When you can mark the surface of the candle by pushing your thumb-nail into it easily, roll the candle hard across the glitter a few times; don't try to get too much glitter to stick to the candle or you may affect the way it burns.

▶▶ Special Effects – ◀◀ the Easy Way!

▷ Yule Log ◁

Did you know that if you have a log fire at Christmas, you can create a special effect by putting lots of ordinary table salt on one of the logs before placing it in the fire.

It will burn with a spectacular and beautiful yellow flame. You can stick salt on the log using thick wallpaper paste. Mix up the paste and then let it dry for an hour until it becomes tacky. Then cover the log with the paste and sprinkle salt all over it.

Simple Christmas Stars

There is one very easy way to make
Christmas stars which can be used on the
tree or added to other decorations.

Cut out two triangles from card or paper.
Cut a slit up from the base of both of them.

Slide them together and add a touch of glue
if necessary.

They will look even better if you use gold
or silver paper, or card that has had some
glitter glued on it. You can spray the finished
star with car paint if you like. Do this in the
garden!

Frosty Fir Cones

Here's a nice job. Go out and collect some
good big fir cones. They usually start falling
from about October onwards – look under fir
trees!

Bring the cones home and leave them in
the garage or somewhere like that, to dry.

Using an aerosol car paint, spray them white (or silver, or gold) and, while they are still wet, roll them in some silver glitter.

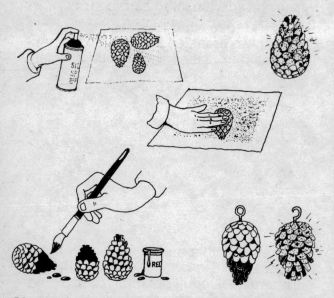

Alternatively they will look very festive if you paint the tips of the cones red, using a soft paint brush.

If you screw a small curtain wire hook or eye into the back of the cones, they are then very easy to add to your Christmas tree or other decorations.

▷ Cartoon Balloons ◁

Balloons look better if you add things to them! Ordinary round balloons can be turned into heads by drawing faces on them. Blow the balloons up first, and then get to work with felt-tip pens!

You can add ears and hair, beards, moustaches and glasses using paper, wool or straw.

What about drawing cartoons of members of the family!

There are some more ideas for caricaturing your guests on the next pages.

▶▶ **Personalise the Party!** ◀◀

Anything you can do to make a Christmas party feel special to the people coming to it will make it more successful! Here are a couple of ways to personalise a party.

▷ Place markers ◁

When you have helped to lay the table for a main meal, find out where everyone is going to sit, then make little 'tent cards' with names on them.

These will help people to find their places, but you can also have fun by illustrating them in such a way that they represent the guest! If someone plays the piano, smokes a pipe, likes fishing, or drinks beer, illustrate the place markers with felt-tip drawings of a keyboard, a pipe, a fishing rod or a pint of beer!

This will get the meal off to a jolly start – at a time when people doing the cooking are probably feeling a bit tense!

Carved Soap

(Christmas in hospital is never quite as good as Christmas at home.) You can carve portraits of one or two of the people coming to stay, and surprise them when they use the bathroom!

Did you know that you can carve soap! It's easy. Make sure the bar is dry – a new one is best – and use a small kitchen knife. You can use a penknife, but be very careful if it is the type that could close on your fingers. (Christmas in hospital is never quite as good as Christmas at home.) You can carve portraits of one or two of the people coming to stay, and surprise them when they use the bathroom!

Make Your Own Silent Crackers

The only really difficult thing about making your own crackers is putting the 'cracker' into them. It is technically possible to buy the strips that go 'crack' in crackers, but it's very difficult to do: there are only a few suppliers, and they can't easily be sent through the post because they are explosives and people might think they were letter bombs!

The simple way round this tricky problem is to make silent crackers, and shout BANG when you pull them!

▷ Very Simple Crackers ◁

Very Simple Christmas Crackers look like any other sort of Christmas cracker but they are not very good for pulling. They are ideal however as a posh way to wrap up small presents like pens, key rings, bottles of perfume, or – if you are a millionaire – diamond rings. (If you are a millionaire it may be easier to just go out and buy your Christmas crackers anyway.)

The important thing when making your own Very Simple Christmas Crackers is to remember to START EARLY. This is because each cracker uses at least one toilet roll middle!

If you want to work out when to start saving toilet roll middles you need to know: a) How many very simple crackers you want to make and b) How many toilet rolls your family uses in a week!

Put your present, and a joke or riddle (see page 61) inside the middle of a toilet roll tube.

Lie the tube on a piece of crêpe paper about 30cm long. Make sure that the crinkly lines in the paper go along the tube, not across it.

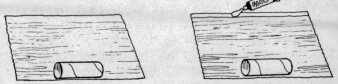

Put glue along the top edge of the paper.

Roll up the toilet roll!

Make the two twists at each end of the cracker like this: push a spare toilet roll tube into one end of the cracker until it nearly touches the one in the middle. Leave a gap of about 5cm.

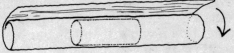

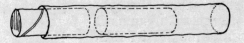

Use some string to nip the end, and pull the spare tube out again. Now do the same to the other end of the cracker. A twist or two will help to give the cracker a professional finish.

▷ Not Quite So Simple Crackers ◁

The disadvantage of the Very Simple Christmas Cracker, apart from the need to save toilet roll middles, is that the tube is rather heavy and makes the cracker feel rather home-made.

The way round this is to make a tube the same size as a toilet roll middle, but from a piece of thinner card. Simply roll it, then proceed as above.

You can also do more to decorate your crackers. You can give them nice frilly edges by pinching the crêpe paper at the ends to stretch it:

Then you can stick gold and silver shiny paper in rings or patterns on the outside. This can strengthen the middle and the ends of the cracker and this will help to ensure that it tears at one of its twists, like a well-behaved cracker is supposed to do.

If you have a large present to give
someone, you can always construct a jumbo-
sized cracker to put it in! Make the central
drum from stoutish card, and do your best to
make it look cracker-like.

▷ Riddles and Jokes for Crackers ◁

If you are making your own crackers (see
page 58) you will need some really tricky
riddles: or you can just use these to test your
friends. You could even perform them with a
partner in front of an audience!
How do ghosts like their eggs.
  Petrifried!

What did the electrician's wife say to him
when he came home from the pub?
  Wire you insulate?!

What do you give an octopus for Christmas?
  Four pairs of gloves.

What does a duck-billed platypus have that
other mammals don't?
  Little duck-billed platypusses!

61

What's white and fluffy and swings through the jungle?

A Meringue-ootang!

What's yellow, tastes of almonds, goes on Christmas cakes, and swings through the jungle?

Tarzanipan!

Why are owls cleverer than chickens?

Have you ever seen Kentucky Fried Owl?!

What do you strain the cabbage with on
Christmas morning?
An advent colander.

What's bigger upside down?
The number 6.

When is it unlucky to see a black cat?
When you're a mouse!

Why don't you
shave your cat?
*Because most
cats prefer
Whiskas!*

What can you put into your left hand but not
in your right hand?
Your right elbow.

What do Red Indians put
under their arms?
Scalpum powder!

What do you get if you
cross a motorway
with a roller-skate?
Run over.

What do you get
if you cross a pet
bird with a fierce
dog?
A budgerigrrrr!

How do you learn to be a dustman?
*You don't; you just pick it up as you go
along.*

Due to industrial action by the NUJ – National
Union of Jesters, there is no joke in this
cracker!

▶▶ **Make Your Own** ◀◀
Christmas Wrapping Paper

They say that giving presents is even nicer
than receiving them (you don't have to agree
with them).
    One way, however, to make giving
presents even more enjoyable is to wrap
them up in paper that you have decorated
yourself. You can even personalise the way
you wrap things up.
    Let's start with a couple of very easy ways
to make special wrapping paper.

▷   Make It Glitter   ◁

You can easily make Christmas paper that
sparkles. Start with plain-coloured paper
which you can buy. If you would like to save
money – and therefore have more to spend
on the presents themselves – you can use old
bits of wallpaper instead (look in the
cupboard under the stairs, or anywhere that
your parents usually leave in a mess).

Spread some glue thinly over the surface of the paper, either in random patterns or in the shape of stars etc., and then sprinkle Christmas glitter over it. The type of glue that comes in a stick is by far the best for this.

You can use the stick like a pen, and can actually write the person's name on the paper with it. It may be best to do this after you have wrapped up the present. The glittering name looks very impressive! I find that silver or gold on red paper looks the most Christmassy.

▷ ## Stencils ◁

Christmas stencils can be bought quite cheaply and are usually used to make pictures on the window-panes with artificial snow. Using spray paint, or a stippling brush, you can use them to improve plain wrapping paper.

You can add a personal touch to the presents you give by decorating the outer wrapping with pictures from magazines. For instance, if you are giving Uncle Fred some pipe tobacco (get Mum or Dad to buy it because you have to be over 18!) you could decorate the wrapping with pictures from tobacco advertisements of gentlemen smoking pipes and looking contented.

One of the most effective applications of this idea is on gramophone records. An LP cover has a good large square area and there are lots of pictures of favourite pop stars that are easy to cut out from pop mags or papers.

Think about every present you are giving, and see if you can decorate the wrapping appropriately.

You can make very nice little name labels for your presents using symmetrical Christmas shapes. Here is how to make very easy holly leaves:

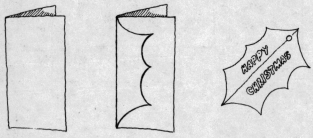

Snowmen name-tags are also simple to draw and cut out:

Once you have made the blank labels you can decorate them with felt-tip pens, and write the lucky person's name on them!

▶▶ **Make Your Own Christmas Cards** ◀◀

There are several ways of making your own Christmas cards, and they will all save you money! They will also mean that your cards are personal and unique.

▷ Simple Cards ◁

The simplest cards are simply made from folded paper.

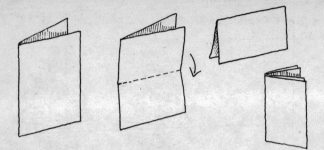

You can then decorate them with crayons, paints or felt-tip pens. Most Christmas images are quite easy to draw:

▷ Cut-out Cards ◁

A card that isn't rectangular is eye-catching in any mantelpiece collection. Here's an easy one in the shape of a Christmas tree. Fold a piece of card or stiff paper in half and draw the outline of a Christmas tree on it. Cut round your outline and open the card out.

You can then decorate it on both sides.

Once you get into the swing of it you can make quantities of these cards in no time!

▷ Reusing Old Christmas Cards ◁

You can easily make very nice Christmas cards using ones that you received last year. What you do is to cut the pictures off the fronts of the old cards and re-mount them on coloured card of your own.

It's advisable to cut out the pictures first and then decide what size and shape of new base card you think will look best. You make the base cards simply by cutting them out from a sheet of bought card or stiff paper.

You can then decorate the inside of the card.
If you find lettering difficult to do, see if you
can find the letters you need in magazines or
papers, cut them out and stick them in – like
a kidnapper's note!

Games For One and All

No party is complete without some games. There are two types of games you can play at Christmas – noisy and quiet! Here is a small selection of both kinds.

▶▶ Racing Games ◀◀

Racing games are almost always noisy and usually need a whole room fairly clear of furniture. They are often more suitable for Christmas afternoons or early evening, and are one way of making sure that Dad doesn't fall asleep!

A long thin room obviously makes the best race-track, but you can always lengthen the course by making competitors go across a room and back again, or across and back as many times as you feel appropriate! (You might even be able to play some of these outside, as long as it isn't snowing.)

Everyone knows what a race is, but here are a few Christmas events that even Sebastian Coe may not have tried.

▷ Newspaper Race ◁

Each 'runner' is given two sheets of newspaper. They stand on one sheet and

hold the other. When the race starts they put
the sheet they are holding in front of them
and step on it, picking up the second one and
then stepping on that – and so on. If anyone
falls or steps off their newspaper they are
instantly declared to have been eaten by
crocodiles. First one to the finishing-line is
the winner!

▷ ## Peanut Race ◁

Everyone is given a peanut and a matchstick.
They get down on hands and knees and the
idea is to propel the peanut across the room
using only the match. On a thick carpet this
can take ages! Make sure you give everyone
the same size nut, or there may be a
stewards enquiry, and 'plain' rather than
roasted are best because they are cleaner.

  If you want to make them work *really*
hard you make them hold the match in their
teeth!

Cigarette Race ◁

This is not a smoking race! Actually it's similar to the peanut race, except that this time you give the runners a cigarette and a rolled-up newspaper. They have to make the cigarette roll along the floor simply by hitting the carpet *behind* it with the paper. They must not hit the cigarette itself.

This game is great fun because it's very difficult to stay in your own lane! You will also find that some competitors favour a few mighty blows on the carpet, often destroying their newspaper in the process, while crafty ones use lots of rapid litle taps to get the cigarette bowling along!

If there are no cigarettes in your house
(Hurrah!) try the Dried Pea Derby:

▷   Dried Pea Derby   ◁

This can be run exactly like the cigarette
race above but you use dried peas instead
(or you can use peanuts, or table tennis balls
– or anything like that). The dried peas can
be propelled using newspapers, or they can
be raced simply by blowing. I think
newspapers are best because blowing hard
gives some people headaches.

▷   Dried Pea Grand National   ◁

A Dried Pea Grand National is totally
different from a Dried Pea Derby! In the
Grand National every runner needs a nice
round dried pea and a drinking straw. They
get down on their hands and knees and have
to race across a room – and back again if you
think they are up to it – holding the peas on
the end of the straw by sucking. The fun
starts when they need to breathe! Anyone
dropping their pea has, of course, to suck it
back on to the end of their straw.

Marble Arch

For a Marble Arch Race the runners are on their knees again, though it can be run standing up if outside. The runners run on their knees carrying a marble between two pencils. If the marble touches their hand they must stop. The race is started with competitors holding two pencils in one hand, the marble on the floor in front of them.

Ice Cream Rally

Here's a race that is good to watch as well as take part in. The contestants are in pairs, and it's best to simply race one pair against another, so that only four people are taking part.

On two chairs, place saucers with ice cream on them (or you can use cold baked beans or cold mashed potato). The

75

contestants kneel on either side of their chair, and each has the handle of a teaspoon in their mouth.

The contestants feed each other and the winning pair are the ones who finish their ice cream first. The real problem of course is that it's difficult to eat when you've got the handle of a teaspoon in your mouth, let alone feed someone else. Be prepared for a mess!

▶▶ Moderately Quiet Games ◀◀

These are what you would probably call 'party games', you can play them in your living-room or dining-room but you won't need to clear away any furniture.

Some of them need some preparation beforehand.

▷ ## Paper Tearing ◁

There are all kinds of paper-tearing games

and most people enter them wholeheartedly. Give everyone a sheet of newspaper and allow them exactly one minute to tear out the shape of a giraffe! The results will probably be hilarious!

A variation of this simple game is to play it in the evening, with all the lights out. Anything with four legs is bound to win!

Of course you can make it easier by choosing easier shapes. A snowman is good, so is a Christmas tree, though even then you'll be surprised at how bad some of the results are!

▷ Games with Magazines ◁

Here are three moderately quiet games you can organise so long as you have saved a really good selection of colour magazines from the Sunday papers.

▷ Name the Event! ◁

A very interesting game is to take supplements that go back over most of the year. Cut out news pictures from them and number the cuttings. Then spread them out round the room and ask people to record on paper what they think the event was. News magazines are a good source of pictures for this competition, and so are ordinary black and white photos from newspapers – but you have to make sure they go back a good long way. About fifteen pictures are usually enough.

Family Album

This is a fun game for younger people. All you need is a large pile of old magazines, a few pairs of scissors and some paste. You give each competitor, or pair of competitors, large cheap scrapbooks in which you have put headings such as: The person I shall marry; Where I shall live; Our first child; My mother; My mother-in-law; Our pet; Me at work.

THE PERSON I SHALL MARRY | WHERE I SHALL LIVE | OUR FIRST CHILD | MY MUM

Then all the contestants have to do is rummage through the magazines to find funny and unlikely pictures. They cut them out and stick them in their albums. The results can be very funny!

▷ Spot the Advert ◁

Cut out advertisements from colour magazines and also remove the names of the product. Number them and stick them up round the living-room – or the whole house if you think people need a bit of exercise. Contestants go round and write down the names of the product being advertised, if

78

they know them. It soon shows you which ads
are effective!

▶▶ Quiet Games Round ◀◀
a Table

Quiet games are important at Christmas.
They are very good for playing round a table
after a big meal. Make sure no one falls
asleep! Here are just a few.

▷ Dentists ◁

At the end of a Christmas meal, in amongst
the pulled cracker paper and nut shells on
the table, there's usually some orange or
tangerine peel. Challenge anyone to make a
really good pair of goofy false teeth with it –
all they need is a knife. It's very easy, so
there are no prizes, but there can be a lot of
laughs.

Kim's Game

This is a traditional memory game, and it's very popular and easy to play. Put a tray on the table with lots of bits and bobs on it – things like a teaspoon, pencil, toy soldier, rubber band – the sort of thing you can usually find in any kitchen drawer. Between twenty and thirty things is about the right number. Cover the tray and its contents with a tea towel.

Tell the contestants that they are going to have exactly a minute to look at the tray and memorise what's on it. (No note-taking allowed of course.)

After one minute, remove the tray and swiftly give out paper and pencils. Give them two minutes to write their lists – the longest accurate one is the winner. (To learn a trick to help you win see the Man Of Mystery's Marvellous Memory Trick on p. 89.)

Give out pieces of paper with this blank 'crossword' on it.

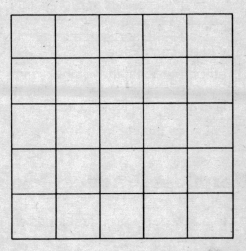

The aim is to build as many words as you can on your own grid, reading down and across as in a crossword puzzle. You do this by calling out letters round the table. When it is your turn, you obviously call out a letter that you need to make a word, but everyone has to put your letter somewhere on their grid, and you have to put theirs on yours!

The game finishes when the grids are full, and the person with the most real words is the winner.

Get a cloth bag – a shoe bag, sponge bag or pillow case will do. Put lots of things in it like sweets, a pencil, marble, coin – things with quite distinctive shapes.

Give everyone a pencil and paper. Then give each of them exactly 30 seconds to feel it and remember what they think is in it. While they write down their thoughts the next person has a try. The longest accurate list is the winner.

▸▸ Harmless Practical Jokes ◂◂

Here are a few party practical jokes where no one will get hurt, not fatally at least, and all the spectators have a good giggle.

▷ Walk The Egg Minefield ◁

Here's a lovely trick which you can play quite safely on anyone, even your Dad.

You clear an area of the floor and space out on it about a dozen eggs, dotted along an imaginary pathway, like this:

Now select your victim. Tell them that the
object is for them to walk along the egg mine-
field blindfolded, and in stocking-feet,
without treading on the eggs. Let them stand
at the start of the pathway first, without the
blindfold, and try to memorise eggsactly
where the eggs are!

When they say they are ready someone
takes them out of the room to blindfold them
and take off their shoes. While this is being
done you are up to some dirty work! Remove
all the eggs and put down instead lots and
lots of little piles of cornflakes.

In comes the poor victim, blindfolded. The
audience try not to laugh. He or she starts to
walk and before very long steps on a little
heap of cornflakes! As you can imagine, in
stocking-feet, the crunch the flakes make
feels just as if he's trodden on an egg!
Everyone howls with mirth and calls out
things like 'Oh no! The carpet!' etc.

This trick always works!

Ask for a volunteer who wants to go on a submarine ride; say that you can reproduce the exact feelings of a magical underwater journey.

Some poor soul will volunteer. Lie him down on the carpet, on his back (of course it may be a 'her'). Then, using an old coat, construct your submarine, like this:

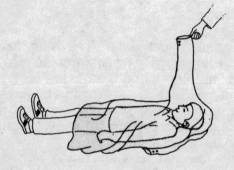

Make sure that the victim can see up the 'periscope' – the sleeve of the coat. Then say, 'Are you ready?' 'Yes' they will say. Your next dramatic little speech then goes something like this:

'Right, we have cast off the ropes from the jetty in the harbour, and your mighty diesel engines are slowly turning. Can you feel the vibrations? We are now turning out into the estuary and heading for the sea . . . You give the order to start the dive. All the hatches are being closed . . . You begin your descent into the murky depths of the ocean . . . Now you are clear of the land, and your submarine is below the waves – all except the periscope. The electric engines are now operating: you are going to dive to the sea bed! Down, down . . . down; only the tip of your periscope is showing. Soon you will be submerged completely. Down, down . At last your periscope is beneath the water . . .'

At this moment you pour a glass of water down the coat-sleeve which, with luck, your submariner will get full in the face!

Then run.

▷   Phantom Aeroplane Ride   ◁

Phantom Aeroplane Ride

You need to do this trick with care. Offer an aeroplane ride to a youngster in the family – a child of seven or eight usually works well. You need someone of about your size to help you as well – though someone bigger would do.

Blindfold your brave pilot and stand them on a chair or low stool. Then you and your helper prepare to lift the chair, and the pilot puts his hands on your heads to steady himself, like this:

You then tell your pilot that you are going to fly him up through the ceiling! What you actually do is this: you lift the chair only an centimetre or so off the floor, but you and your accomplice slowly lower your heads.

This gives the victim the most powerful feeling that he is way above your heads. You can of course give him a running commentary as the flight proceeds! 'You are now at cloud level, and heading out over the sea. Below you, you can just make out tiny dots of fishing boats etc. etc. . . .'

Slowly bring him back down by raising your heads again, or alternatively tell him to take his blindfold off! he will get quite a surprise when he finds he is only a centimetre off the ground!

(If you want to feel how strong the illusion of going up is in this trick, get two friends to try it out on you.)

▶▶ Games That Turn Out To ◀◀ Be Practical Jokes!

Here are a couple of practical jokes that start off just like Christmas party games. Audiences love them!

▷ Boat Race ◁

For this you need a metal tea-tray or flat baking-tray – it must be waterproof – and a jug of water and two matchsticks. Pick two contestants and invite them to take part in a boat race.

Place the tray on the floor (not on the best carpet – you'll see why in a minute). Fill it with water; you don't need very much, just enough to cover the bottom of the tray.

Get the contestants to kneel down opposite each other across the tray, and tell them that the game is to blow a matchstick– which represents a boat – across to the other side of the tray.

Let one of them decide to be Oxford, and the other Cambridge. Tell them they can't start until you say go. They will get very excited! They will lean right down close to the water's edge ready to get their matchstick boats off to a really good start.

Here comes the joke! You say 'Ready, Steady' and on the word 'GO!' you smack your hand down in the middle of the tray, and they get a face full of water!

Health Warning: My brother-in-law did this trick once and the lady who was Oxford picked up the tray and hit him on the head with it. The next trick is even worse.

▷   Crack An Egg   ◁

You need a wicked accomplice for this joke. You challenge someone in the family – Dad perhaps? – to an 'egg-spoon duel'.

You and he sit opposite each other on chairs, knees almost touching. You each have the handle of a teaspoon in your mouth. Explain to your opponent that all you are going to do to each other is take turns at trying to hit each other on the head with the spoons in your mouths. In case he's a bit worried about it, let him have the first go. Assure him he won't get hurt.

Now the point is that it's quite impossible to hit someone on the head at all hard with a teaspoon held in your mouth. So you lean forward slightly to let him have a crack at you, and when he's tried you tell him to lean forward to let you have a go.

He does, but what he doesn't know is that your wicked accomplice is right behind him, and at exactly the right moment gives him a sharpish tap on the nut with a spoon!

Dad then thinks it *is* possible to crack *you* on the nut after all and tries again! Again he fails, but when you do it you seem to be able to give him quite a nifty tap!

The audience, knowing what is going on, usually collapses in hysterics at about this point. Be prepared to run for it when Dad finally rumbles what's going on!

Just a word of warning – don't play this trick on anyone who is bald. Without hair to protect them this could hurt!

Your Christmas audience will be willing to be puzzled and amazed as well as amused. All the following tricks are very easy to do – no skill needed!

▶▶ Man of Mystery's ◀◀ Marvellous Memory Trick

Here is a Christmas trick that will make all your family and friends think you are *very* clever! Once you know how to do it, you will be able to memorise twenty-one objects, and the order in which they are given to you.

You will need to dress up as a wise man – perhaps with a turban on your head, and introduce yourself as the Man of Mystery with a Marvellous Memory. Then sit cross-legged on the floor and get someone to blindfold you. It's important that they do this well, because being blindfolded will help you to concentrate.

You then ask members of the audience to call out any object they like – it doesn't matter what it is – and when you are ready, ask for another one. You will go on for up to twenty-one objects, and then, hey presto, you will immediately be able to list all twenty-one objects in the order they gave them to you –

number one, a hairbrush, number two, a clothes-hanger etc.

This is how you do it. It isn't really a trick because you do actually memorise all the objects, but you use a special device to help you that never fails.

First of all you need to work out in your own mind a very simple code to remind you of the numbers one to twenty-one – my own one is printed opposite.

Let's say that, like me, you can always associate the number two with Adam and Eve, and eleven with people playing cricket. All you then do is imagine hard a scene or picture linking the object you are given with your own code. If, for instance, number two really was a coat-hanger, imagine Adam handing Eve a coat-hanger! Pause to make sure you can really see it in your mind's eye. The more ridiculous the scene you 'see' the better – perhaps Eve is looking very cross because she has no clothes to hang on it! When at the end of the session you have to remember what object number two was, it's very easy. Two = Adam and Eve, and you instantly remember the image of them and the clothes-hanger! So two is a coat-hanger.

Try it – you'll be amazed at how easy it is, but it is absolutely essential that you can remember your code of number associations instantly.

This is my own code: I've never made a mistake doing this memory feat!

1 = God
2 = Adam and Eve
3 = The three ball sign of a
    pawnbroker's shop
4 = People playing bridge (cards)
5 = People playing the game of 'fives'
6 = People picking up sticks – as in five,
    six, pick up sticks
7 = The Severn Bridge
8 = People eating (ate)
9 = A German soldier saying 'No'
10 = Green Bottles
11 = People playing cricket
12 = The Twelve Apostles
13 = A black cat – unlucky
14 = Maids Courting! (thirteen, fourteen
     maids a'courting)
15 = People playing rugger
16 = Kitchen – it nearly rhymes!
17 = Just 17 magazine
18 = A birthday cake – it's an important
     birthday
19 = Queen Victoria – I use her because
     she was reigning in 1900.
20 = A van – it sounds a bit like the
     French for twenty.
21 = A key – you used to get one when
     you were twenty-one.

Of course you don't need to use my code –
build one of your own and get to know it
back to front!
    One of your audience will need a pencil
and paper to write the objects down and
check your skill.

▶▶ **Conjuring Tricks To Do** ◀◀

To be a good conjuror takes hours of
practice, and often some specialised
equipment. You won't need either to do
these!

▷   Disappearing Matches   ◁

You can even make money with this trick,
though you'll get rich very slowly!
   Start by fixing a matchbox with a few
matches in it up your right arm, under your
sleeve. You can keep it in place with
sellotape or an elastic band. Then get two
empty matchboxes.
   Tell the audience that one box has got
matches in it, the other is empty. (This is a lie,
but conjurors always tell lies – they're
allowed to!)
   Pick one box up with your left hand and
shake it: silence. Pick the other box up with
your right hand and shake it. The matches in
the box up your sleeve rattle, so the
audience – poor fools – think that the box in
your right hand has got matches in it.
   Then shuffle the boxes vigorously, crossing
them over many times on the table.
Challenge anyone to say which is the box
with matches in it! They'll be wrong of course
– both are empty. You can't lose; anyway, not
until some clever dick rumbles how you do
it!

Crafty Coin Trick

Here's another trick which can earn you money. Ask your audience to lend you two pound coins and a twenty-pence coin. Place them in a row on a table with a cloth on it, and put a glass on the top of them like this:

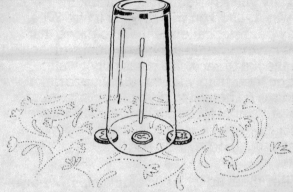

Now suggest to the audience that, if you can get the twenty-pence piece without touching the glass, you can keep it. They'll probably agree – after all it is Christmas.

What you do now is gently scratch the tablecloth next to the glass. The coin will slowly creep towards you!

Drink the Water

This one is half conjuring trick, and half practical joke, so it's ideal for Christmas!

Put a small glass of water on the floor in front of you and put a hat over it. Tell the audience that by special magical powers you will be able to drink the water *without touching the hat*!

Kneel down behind the hat, put your face close to the floor behind it, and make extravagant drinking noises. After a while look up, lick your lips and say, 'There! I told you I could!'

They will say you haven't drunk the glass of water, and you will say you have. When they persist, challenge them to prove that you haven't drunk it. One of them will then lift up the hat to show the glass full of water.

You then simply lift the glass up, drink it, and say, 'There, I told you I could drink the water without touching the hat, and I have!'

▷ ## Blow Your Hat Off! ◁

Cheer them up with this old illusion! Wear a hat with a good strong brim – especially at the back. Stand with your back to a wall. Put your finger in your mouth, cross your eyes and pretend to blow. Your hat lifts up at the front, as if it's being blown off.

What is really happening of course is that you are leaning the back of the brim against the wall and pushing! It looks very funny.

▷ Non-Exploding Balloon ◁

A very effective way of ending a conjuring act is to stick a pin in a balloon without its bursting. Tell your audience that at the end of your show you will be demonstrating to them the world's one and only non-exploding balloon. Have it inflated and ready.

When the time comes, pick up a pin and pop it into the balloon; your audience will scream and put their hands over their ears! The only thing is that your balloon doesn't burst. The reason for this is that you have stuck a small square of sellotape to it, and have stuck the pin into that. The pin merely makes a small hole in the tape and the balloon deflates very slowly. Try it in advance if you don't believe me.

Two things are vital if this trick is going to work: don't let the audience see the sellotape, and make sure you don't miss it with the pin!

Amateur conjuring is often more fun if you add jokes to it. The late comedian Tommy Cooper was quite marvellous at this: actually he was a good conjuror, but he made fun of himself by doing tricks that didn't work. If any of his programmes are repeated on television – watch them!

Try to put jokes into your act:

Did you know that as well as being a
magician I am also a superman? I can jump
as high as the Eiffel Tower. Don't you believe
me?
Audience: 'No!'
Well, I can – you see, the Eiffel Tower *can't
jump*!!

Or this old line:

Please observe before I do this trick that I
have nothing up my sleeve – only an arm,
and there's no 'arm in that, is there?

▷   Sliced Banana   ◁

In between doing conjuring tricks it is most
effective to peel a banana and eat it! The
point is that your banana is ready sliced!

▷ The Easy Way To Do This Trick ◁

Take a banana and a long fine needle.
Pierce the banana skin with the needle and
wiggle it round until you think it has cut
through the banana. Do this several times,
right down the length of the banana – it is
often best to put the needle in on one of the
ridges in the banana skin, or in any dark
patches, but in any case the needle hole
should be completely invisible to your
amazed audience!

The Trickier Way To Do This Trick

You get cleaner, better slices if you do this trick another way, but it takes more time and care. This time actually thread the needle with some cotton. Poke the needle into the banana at one of the 'joints' in the skin and push the head of it along under the skin to the next joint. Bring it out.

Now pass it back in the hole that it's just come out of, and go along to the next joint, and do the same thing. As you can see, you are sewing a circle of cotton round the banana just under the skin.

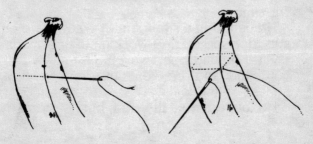

When your needle comes out of the very
first hole, the circle is complete. Pulling both
ends of the cotton now slices the banana very
neatly, and the tiny holes in the banana skin
don't show.

Your audience will be amazed!

▶▶ **A Tricky Story** ◀◀

Here is a horrible puzzle to set people at a
Christmas meal or party. Let's hope nobody
already knows it!

Give your audience paper and pencils.
Then ask them to write a sentence that has
got the word 'and' in it five times. They'll all
begin to say that that's easy, but you must
make it clear that the five 'ands' have got to
be one after the other, with no other words in
between. That will make them struggle!

Don't let them struggle very long. Tell them
the following story to put them out of their
agony.

There was once a pub called the Slug and
Lettuce. The sign outside the pub was very
old and the landlord decided to have it
repainted.

He called in a sign-painter who got up on
a ladder and started work on the new sign.

After he had been working for a few
hours the landlord went outside to see how
he was getting on.

He looked up at the sign, but he didn't

like what he saw: 'I say,' he said to the sign-painter, 'I don't think much of that – it's too difficult to read.'

'Why?' said the man.

'Well,' replied the landlord, 'you haven't left enough space between the Slug and AND and AND and Lettuce!'

There you are, five 'ands' all in a row!

▶▶ A Party Puzzler ◀◀

Here is a trick which will puzzle, baffle and bewilder anyone at a party. You need a trained accomplice to help you.

First of all lay nine books down on the floor in this pattern:

Then announce to the audience that you are going to send your accomplice out of the room, and by using brain power alone you will be able to tell him which book from those on the floor the audience has selected in his absence! Tell them that you are able to do this by special psychic powers that only you and he have!

Send the accomplice out of the room. Then quietly ask a member of the audience to point out one of the books. Make sure all this is done quietly or they may suspect that your accomplice is listening! When all the audience is certain which book is the chosen one, call the accomplice back in.

Using a walking stick, or a pointer, you are going to tell your partner which of the nine books is the one selected. Start by doing some magical nonsense on the floor with the walking stick, drawing a complicated pattern on the carpet. Your audience will be searching all the time for some hidden code. After a while say to your accomplice, 'Have you got it yet?' He will say, 'Yes', which is a lie!

But then you look at the pattern of books and touch one (not the chosen one) and say, 'Is it this one?'

'No!' says your accomplice. Take your time and touch a couple more. Both times he will say 'no'. This intrigues your audience who think the trick has gone wrong!

Then touch the right book and say, 'Is it this one?' 'Yes!' says your accomplice.

How does he know? Well, when you touch

the very first book, you touch it in the place
that indicates where in the pattern the
selected book is. For instance, if your
audience has chosen the book in the middle
of the nine, you touch the first book right in
the middle of its cover; if it's the one in the
top left corner, that's where you touch the
cover of the first book.

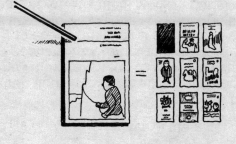

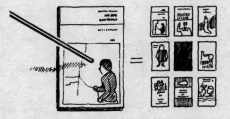

The audience always think they know how
it's done – they usually think it's something to
do with your voice and they'll make you do it
again and again to check their theories!
They'll even volunteer to be your
accomplice and get hopelessly stuck! Little
do they know how simple it is!

▶▶ **Crafty Card Tricks** ◀◀

Let's start with the oldest, worst and nastiest card trick in the world!

▷ ## Pick Up Fifty-Two ◁

Get an unsuspecting volunteer and tell them you are going to show them how to do a card trick called Pick Up Fifty-Two. Hold a pack of cards against the side of any piece of furniture – a chair or table, for instance.

Tell the volunteer to take over from you, and to hold the cards using only their thumb, like this:

Then tell them to say
the magic Christmas
spell:

Ivy Holly
I'm a wally

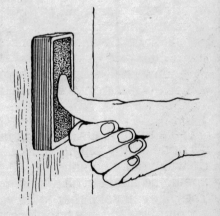

Now tell them to remove their thumb. All the cards, of course, fall on the floor. 'There you are!' you say with a jolly smile. 'I told you you'd learn how to pick up fifty-two – there's fifty-two cards to pick up!'

Special note: Always pick a victim smaller than you!

And now some proper card tricks:

▷   Pick A Card!   ◁

There are lots of 'pick a card' tricks, and most of them don't require any skill.

▷   The Classic Version   ◁

Tell one of your audience to take a card from those fanned in your hand and look at it without letting you see it. Tell them to make really sure that they know what it is, and get them to show it to the rest of the audience as well. While they are all concentrating on the card they won't be concentrating on you.

Meanwhile, you hold half the pack in each hand. In your right hand is half the pack, lying face down on your palm, and in your left hand is the rest of the pack held from above. Take a sneaky look at the face of the bottom card in your left hand.

Get the member of the audience to replace the card on the top of the pile in your right hand, and then unite the pack.

Starting at the top, peel off the cards until you come to the one that was on the bottom of the left-hand pile. The next card is the one that was picked.

Special tip: When you put the pack together DON'T SHUFFLE IT!!!

▷ Extra Sneaky Version ◁

Tell your audience that you can tell what a card is by reading it through your finger-tips. Get someone in the audience to pick a card and give it to you without your being able to see the front of it. Hold it up so that they can all see it and you can't. Read it with your finger!

Put the card face down in the pack, but give it a fairly sharp squeeze as you do, so that you bend it slightly.

Put the rest of the cards back on top of it. The bent card will lift them very slightly so that you will be able to feel the division even if no one can see it. You'll easily find the card again, and amaze the audience when you identify it.

▷ ## Just As Sneaky Version ◁

Take an old pack of cards that nobody wants any more. Reduce the width of them at one end by carefully sandpapering the whole pack.

Hold a fan of cards up to a member of the audience and invite them to take a card, to look at it, and to put it back. While they are looking at the card you show the audience that you are shuffling the pack. Then make a fan again and tell the person to put the card back, anywhere.

What they have not spotted is that when you had finished shuffling the cards you turned the pack round. When they put the card back, and you close the pack down to a neat pile, their card will be obvious to touch because it is the wrong way round in the tapered pack. You can feel its edges. You can even produce it for them without looking – with the pack behind your back!

Longer Jokes

The ability to tell longer jokes is *very* impressive.

The main thing is that you have got to learn them! The effect is ruined if you have to look at notes or read from a paper. You don't need to use exactly these words; however, it will help to hold an audience's attention if you use actions that are appropriate to the story. For instance, you can demonstrate how the gorilla walks into the pub in this first joke – make your arms look nice and long.

▶▶ Gorilla In A Pub ◀◀

A gorilla walked into a pub. He sidled up to the bar, his hairy knuckles dragging on the ground, and asked the barman for a pint of beer.

The barman thought he was on to a good thing, so he gave him a pint, and said, 'Five pounds, please.' The gorilla opened his wallet and gave the barman five pounds. Then he sat on a bar stool and sipped his beer.

The pub wasn't very busy, and eventually the barman, who was rather fascinated at having a gorilla in his pub, thought he'd get talking to it.

'We don't get many gorillas in here, you know,' he said.

'I'm not surprised, with beer at five quid a pint!' said the gorilla.

▶▶ **Three-Legged Turkeys** ◀◀

A farmer once had a very bright idea. He thought he would breed a new sort of turkey that would make him a fortune at Christmastime. He knew that everyone liked the legs on a Christmas turkey, and so he decided to try to breed a turkey with THREE legs.

Well, he went into his turkey-house and spent months and months there until – low and behold – he got his turkeys to produce eggs that hatched into little turkeys that had three legs!

A few weeks later, a friend of his came out to the turkey-house. He had not seen the farmer recently and he wanted to know what he had been doing with himself.

'What have you been up to?' the friend asked.

'Well!' said the farmer. 'I have been very clever. For months and months, I have struggled to produce turkeys with three legs for the Christmas market, and a few weeks ago I managed it. Look at all these young birds.'

The friend looked into one of the pens, and was amazed. 'Are they any good to eat?' he asked.

'I don't know,' said the farmer. 'I haven't managed to catch one yet!'

▶▶ **Toilet Water!** ◀◀

Here's another longish joke that you can tell, or you could adapt it as a sketch for two people:

A man was looking very miserable, and his friend asked him what the matter was.

'I haven't got any girl-friends,' said the man. 'Women don't seem to find me very attractive.'

'Well,' said his friend. 'If I were you I'd take a bit more trouble with my appearance. I'd get a nice new white shirt, and some smart new trousers, and a posh tie. Then I'd get my hair cut, and have a shave, and put aftershave on my chin and some toilet water behind my ears.'

The man thanked his friend and off he went.

The friend saw him again a week later. He was looking much smarter, but he had a big bandage round his head, and a glum look on his face.

'What's the matter with you?' he asked.

'Well,' said the man, 'I did all those things you suggested. I bought a new white shirt, and some new trousers and a posh tie. I had a hair cut and shave, but no girls will go out with me with this bandage round my head . . .'

'Why have you got a bandage round your head?' his friend asked.

'Well, when I tried to put the toilet water behind my ears the seat fell down and cracked me on the head!'

A Potted Panto For Four Performers

The ultimate Christmas entertainment is of course the pantomime. There is no reason why you can't put one on in your own house, and the following script should help you to do so.

All you need for a stage is the end of a room with a door in it that you can use as an entrance and exit. Have a good look round the house to decide where the best place is for putting on a play. Sometimes hallways are good, especially if your audience can make use of the stairs as well as chairs.

I have written this panto for four actors. Fortunately there is a tradition in pantomime that girls can take boys' roles – usually the hero – and boys can take girls' – usually the 'dame'. This means that the script below can be done by four girls, four boys or any sort of mixture! It doesn't really matter how you hand out the parts, but it can be fun if the Ugly Sister is played by someone bigger than the others; she (or he!) could certainly be bigger than Prince Charming.

If more actors want to take part you will have to invent some more characters. Prince Charming could have an assistant called Dandini, and you could easily give Cinderella a very bossy mother!

The main thing is to rehearse really well, and to add family jokes wherever possible. Treat my script as a starting-point, and do some funny script-writing of your own. Make the costumes as outrageous as you can, and put lots of energy into the show. You can't go wrong!

CINDERELLA

The players:
Cinderella
Buttons
Ugly Sister
Fairy Godmother who also plays **Prince Charming.**

*Enter **Cinderella** in tatty clothes and with a glum expression on her face. She sits down.*

Cinders: Oh dear, here I sit in the cinders with only Buttons and my ugly sister for company. I've got no money – why, I can't even afford *two* ugly sisters!

*Enter **Buttons**, cheerfully.*

Buttons: Hallo, Cinders! You look about as cheery as a turkey on Christmas Eve! Cheer up! I've got good news for you – Prince Charming is having a disco up at the palace!

Cinders: Oh Buttons, we're undone! My ugly sister will get an invitation and marry the Prince and live happily ever after, and I'll be made to do all their housework like a poor little skivvy.

Buttons: Fear not, Cinders! I've got an invite for you here! *He waves a big white envelope towards her.*

*Enter **Ugly Sister**, snatching invite out of Button's hand.*

Ugly Sister: Ta very much, Buttons – you little twit – I'll have that!

Cinderella: How dare you, you big bully! You're worse than two ugly sisters put together!

Ugly Sister: Look, Cinders! I fancy going to the disco and hooking the prince! My looks will enchant him! He will make an excellent husband for me. If it will stop you making a

114

silly fuss here's some beans in return for the invite! *Gives tin of baked beans to Cinders!*

*Exit **Ugly Sister**, who changes into something posh for her next entrance.*

Buttons: Oh goodie, Cinders! Baked beans – my favourite food!

Cinders: Don't be an idiot, Buttons. Sometimes you are so thick I think I'll replace you with a zip! What good are beans?! I'm going to throw them out of the window! Off you go to bed, Buttons, while I sleep here in the ashes!

*Exit **Buttons**. Cinders 'throws beans out of the window' by placing them off stage, and lies down to sleep.*

*Enter **Fairy Godmother** (extra fun if this is played by a boy – and bear in mind that the same person will be Prince Charming in the next scene.)*

Fairy: Hallo Cinders! I'm your baked bean fairy godmother!

Cinders: You don't look like a fairy

godmother – you look more like Mrs Thatcher! *(or whoever you want to take the micky out of! – Norman Tebbit in drag, Les Dawson, the lady next door . . .!)*

Fairy: Oh there are all sorts of baked bean fairies. We come in fifty-seven varieties! Fear not! You shall go to the disco!

Cinders: How? I haven't got a invitation!

Fairy: Don't fret about that. You will get in just by being the most glamorous, beautiful, gorgeous creature there. Princess Di goes to lots of gigs without an invite!

Cinders: Gosh!

Fairy: Call Buttons – we'll need a few things to help me with a magic spell.

Cinders: Buttons! Buttons!

*Enter **Buttons**.*

Fairy: Ah Buttons, have you got a pumpkin, and some white mice?

Buttons: Oh yes. We've got a pumpkin in the garden, and I'll soon catch some mice. But first, here's a joke! What does a man do standing up that a lady does sitting down, and a dog does on three legs?

Fairy and **Cinders** together: We don't know. What *does* a man do standing up that a lady does sitting down and a dog does on three legs?

Buttons: Shakes hands!

Cinders: Oh, you are fly, Buttons!

Fairy: Right, Buttons, while you are catching those mice and apologising to the audience for that terrible joke, Cinderella and I are going to the palace to the, Prince's disco. Come on, Cinders, if we hurry we'll catch a number 62 bus!

Cinders: Hey! what about a fairy coach and a ball gown and some fairy footmen!

Fairy: Come off it, Cinders! Who do you think I am, Paul blinking Daniels?!

*Exit **Cinders** and **Fairy**.*

*While Buttons is making this next speech **Fairy** has to change quickly into **Prince Charming**!*

Buttons: (*direct this straight to the audience*)

Attend with patience, Ladies and Gents
Our scene we now are shiftin'!
We're off to the palace, big and posh
And we're leaving Cinder's kitchen!

We're sorry we're short on stage effects
We should have gone with a magical flash!
We'd like to have done a bit better
But we're much too short of cash!

Imagine the palace, then, here in this
    room,
With guests – all is glamour and glitter.
Even the Ugly Sister's tried hard
She still looks a wreck – but don't titter!

Exit **Buttons**, *Enter* **Ugly Sister**

Ugly Sister *(dressed up in party clothes, and looking very uncomfortable! Use lots of lipstick etc.):*

So this is the palace so big and so grand
When I'm married I'll live here quite
    willingly!
Cinders can do all the housework.
Blimey these high heels are killing me!

Here comes the Prince, the man of my
    dreams!
He's so cool and so handsome and hip!
I only hope that he asks me to dance.
Cor (*wriggle*) this corset is giving me some
gip!

Enter **Prince Charming**

Prince: I am the Prince, I'm handsome, charming, rich and very modest about it. Tonight I shall choose the girl I shall marry – lucky girl!

Ugly Sister: Eee up, Prince! I'm the one for you! My lips are like petals.

Prince: Yes, bicycle petals!

Ugly Sister: And look at my lovely black hair!

Prince: Very nice – it matches your teeth.

*Enter **Buttons** and **Cinderella.***

Cinders: Oh Buttons, isn't this palace grand! Which one is the Prince?

Prince: I am, and I can see that you are the girl for me. I would like to give you the very great honour of having the next dance with me!

They start to dance to a pop song (Buttons or Ugly Sister will be able to start playing a tape).

Ugly Sister: Buttons, you little rotter, what are you doing here with my sister! Here, dance with me – I may be able to get between them! I'll just take these shoes off!

Ugly Sister takes off her high heel shoes and they dance to the music until it stops. Work out a funny dance for the four of them, with the Ugly Sister doing her best to dance with the Prince. Cinders speaks when the music stops.

Cinders: Thank you, Prince. Very enjoyable; I'll just take my shoes off before the next dance.

Cinders takes her shoes off and puts them with her Ugly Sister's!

Prince: Wait, I think I'm going to make a proclamation! I have chosen the girl for me! I am going to marry the sweet, pretty little girl whose foot fits this crystal slipper!

He goes to the four shoes but picks up one of the Ugly Sister's shoes. The audience should be able to see this mistake, because the Ugly Sister's shoes should be far bigger and more clumpy than Cinderella's!

Buttons: That's not a crystal slipper. It looks more like the Crystal Palace!

Prince: Every girl in the kingdom must try it on.

Ugly Sister: I've been 'trying it on' all night!

*There is now a **tableau** – which is a mime, or little scene, where no words are spoken. You can act this bit as if it's in slow motion. The Prince takes the shoe and tries it on Cinderella's foot. It doesn't fit. Buttons, the Ugly Sister and Cinderella all shake their heads! The Prince is amazed and horrified. The Ugly Sister sees her chance and is very keen to try on the shoe. Of course, her foot fits, Buttons and Cinders have to nod in agreement.*

Prince: Oh no, the shoe fits this great harridan!

Ugly Sister: Hurrah! What day shall we get married on?

The Prince shrugs his shoulders and accepts his fate!

Cinders:
    Though I once thought the Prince was smashing,
    I'm glad the slipper failed to fit.

Though he may have a load of money
He really is a ghastly twit!

He'll suit my sister – she's mutton dressed
as mutton.
And I know that I'll be much better off –
with Buttons!

Cinders and **Buttons** *hold hands, so do*
Prince Charming *and* **Ugly Sister**. *All bow*!

The End

OK, *now* you can turn on the telly again.

You can see more Magnet Books
on the following pages:

SARA LITVINOFF & VIDA ADAMOLI

Front Page Kids

You don't have to be a genius to get into the
newspapers. All the children in this book
have been famous for a day. They either did
something incredibly silly, slightly shocking,
amazingly bizarre, wonderfully brave – or hit
the headlines quite by accident.

Among others, there are the kids whose
school uniform battles hit the news, the girl
who finds a fortune in her fish and chips, the
boy who was a millionaire for a day, and the
one who spent six years in a tent!

GRIDIRON STORIES

LAURENCE AND MATTHEW JAMES

First and Ten

Soccer-mad Dave Sheppard is star striker for his local youth team – and this could be their best season ever! But Dave's friend, Wilburn, persuades him to watch a game of American Football on television. Fascinated by the power and skill of the sport, Dave is thrilled when he gets the chance to try out for a nearby American Football team – until he discovers that it clashes with his soccer team's cup final . . .

Also available:

Second and Five
Third and Goal
Touchdown!

More Fiction from Magnet Books

While every effort is made to keep prices low, it is sometimes necessary to increase prices at short notice. Magnet books reserve the right to show new retail prices on covers which may differ from those previously advertised in the text or elsewhere.

The prices shown below were correct at the time of going to press.

416 95900 8	SHEPHERD'S FLOCK	Elizabeth Gowans	£1.75
416 95420 0	WATCH FOR THE GHOST	Sheila Haigh	£1.50
416 52510 5	THE TEAM THAT WOULDN'T GIVE IN	Michael Hardcastle	£1.50
416 62190 2	TIGER OF THE TRACK	Michael Hardcastle	£1.50
416 79840 3	UNITED	Michael Hardcastle	£1.50
416 04532 4	WINNING RIDER	Michael Hardcastle	£1.75
416 51680 7	THE WICKED ONE	Mollie Hunter	£1.50
416 24820 9	FISHY BUSINESS	Robert Lee	£1.50
416 50130 3	JIMMY ZEST	Sam McBratney	£1.25
416 59720 3	BIRTHDAY BURGLAR & A VERY WICKED HEADMISTRESS	Margaret Mahy	£1.75
416 63780 9	LEAF MAGIC AND FIVE OTHER FAVOURITES	Margaret Mahy	£1.50
416 61670 4	BLUE MISTY MONSTERS	Catherine Sefton	£1.75
416 26510 3	EMER'S GHOST	Catherine Sefton	£1.50
416 61530 9	GHOST GIRL	Catherine Sefton	£1.50
416 26500 6	THE SLEEPERS ON THE HILL	Catherine Sefton	£1.10
416 89440 2	THE FOX HOLE	Ivan Southall	£1.50

All these books are available at your bookshop or newsagent, or can be ordered direct from the publisher. Just tick the titles you want and fill in the form below.

MAGNET BOOKS, Cash Sales Department,
PO Box 11, Falmouth,
Cornwall TR10 9EN.

Please send cheque or postal order, no currency, for purchase price quoted and allow the following for postage and packing:

UK • 60p for the first book, 25p for the second book and 15p for each additional book ordered to a maximum charge of £1.90.

BFPO and Eire 60p for the first book, 25p for the second book and 15p for each next seven books, thereafter 9p per book.

Overseas Customers £1.25 for the first book, 75p for the second book and 28p for each subsequent title ordered.

NAME (Block Letters) ....

ADDRESS ....

....